PUFFIN BOOKS

Editor: Kaye Webb

Something to Make

What can you make with yoghourt pots, bits of shiny paper, scraps of fabric, cotton reels, tinsel string, old Christmas cards, odd bits of wool and ribbon, cardboard rolls, egg boxes, and that kind of stuff?

All sorts of things. Collages for instance, and peg dolls and weather charts, scrap books, potato cuts, a snake to keep out the draughts, a purse with your initials on it, a papier mâché owl (or pirate or Father Christmas), paper flowers, a Christmas stable, a wall plaque, cotton-reel animals, a woolly ball for a baby, a tie and dye handkerchief and a melon-seed necklace.

This is a wonderfully varied and practical collection of things for children to make from the odds and ends around the home, with very little extra outlay of money. The author, Felicia Law, is headmistress of the Unicorn School, Richmond, Surrey. She has taught art and handicrafts, and knows from experience exactly what children can tackle most successfully.

For parents to work with children up to seven, and then for children to discover for themselves.

Something to Make

by Felicia Law

Illustrated by Gunvor Edwards

Penguin Books

Penguin Books Ltd, Harmondsworth,
Middlesex, England
Penguin Books Inc., 7110 Ambassador Road,
Baltimore, Maryland 21207, U.S.A.
Penguin Books Australia Ltd, Ringwood,
Victoria, Australia

First published 1971
Reprinted 1971, 1972 (twice)
Copyright © Felicia Law, 1971
Illustrations Copyright © Gunvor Edwards, 1971

Made and printed in Great Britain by
Cox & Wyman Ltd, London, Reading and Fakenham
Set in Monotype Bembo

CONTENTS

MAKING WITH PAPIER MÂCHÉ

MAKING A WEATHER RECORD

MAKING WITH WOOL

MAKING PATTERNS

MAKING DO WITH ODDS AND ENDS

MAKING A PRINT

MAKING WITH MARZIPAN OR PASTRY

MAKE BELIEVE

MAKING SOUNDS

MAKING FOR CHRISTMAS

ACKNOWLEDGEMENT

My sincere thanks to all my friends and fellow teachers who offered ideas, and particularly to Jennifer Morris for her help with the manuscript itself. Much of the credit, however, goes to young friends and pupils who have enthusiastically and successfully produced everything described in this book.

There are many exciting and interesting things that can be made from the junk and scraps that find their way into your home. Often you see things lying about that straightaway give you ideas. I find this with bits of satin material and buttons, or sometimes with tissue papers or crinkly card. Then I start to hoard my bits and pieces and end up with boxes and boxes of them, just waiting for the moments I am inspired to make something.

If you get ideas about cotton reels, and if you hoard cheese cartons and toffee wrappers and yoghourt pots, you are just the person for this book. If not, start your junk collection today. You will get lots of fun from using it in different ways. Some of my ideas are very straightforward, but I am sure you will gather extra ones and develop and change them as you go along, and perhaps make lots of really exciting things which I haven't even mentioned.

Just one word – do finish making things carefully, and always mount them on card or in a box.

Fragile things might fit nicely inside a polythene bag, so keep them safe that way. Build up a collection of the things you make. Many of them make nice presents and people will always be happy to receive something you have made yourself.

A note about the use of glue

Often flour or wallpaper paste is not strong enough for glueing, and where necessary I have said that strong glue should be used. In these cases a rubber-based glue is best.

MAKING READY

1. Put on your apron and roll up your sleeves.

2. Cover the table with newspaper.

3. Collect together all your materials.

4. When you have finished, tidy everything away and clean up.

MAKING WITH PAPER

Cover a big cardboard box with gaily coloured paper and make it your PAPER BOX.

Then collect together as many different kinds of paper as you can and keep them in your box.

Magazines   Tissue paper
Newspapers   Wallpaper
Silver paper   Used birthday and
Toffee wrappers   Christmas cards.

1. Make a Scrapbook

Stick your 'Making with Paper' ideas into a scrapbook. They will look nicer and keep cleaner if they are mounted, and you will have them all together.

Collect together:

    At least 6 sheets of paper 16 ins. × 12 ins. or larger
    Scissors
    Needle
    Thread.

Now begin:

Make sure all the sheets of paper are the same size, then crease each sheet down the centre by folding in half.

Tie a large knot in the thread, and sew through all the sheets in large stitches up and down the crease (see Fig. 2). Secure thread by knotting it round the last stitch.

Later I will show you how you can decorate your cover (see p. 30).

Fig. 1

Fig. 2

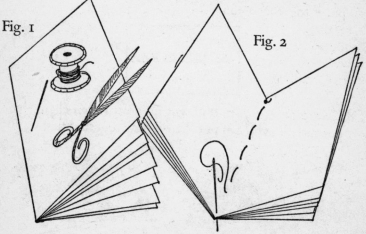

2. Make a Picture Jigsaw

Collect together:

Old cards
Scissors
Envelopes.

Now begin:

Choose an old greetings card with a colourful picture on it.
Now cut it up, with wiggly lines if you can, so that it is divided
up into about twelve pieces. Put the pieces in an envelope so
you don't lose any, and make up a title to write on the envelope.

You have now made your own jigsaw. See how quickly you
can put it together again.

MY RABBIT JIGSAW

If there are two of you, both cut up a card then change envelopes and see who can put their jigsaw together first.

3. Make a Mosaic

Collect together:

Paper Box
Scissors (optional)
Sheet of white paper at least 12 ins. square
Paste
Brush
Pencil.

Now begin:

Draw a wiggly pattern on the sheet of paper. Choose ONE colour, like blue. Fill each space with small TORN pieces of blue paper, blue tissue, blue dotted paper, blue striped paper, blue with writing on it, dark blue, light blue, navy blue or royal blue. Look for blues in magazines.

Do not leave any white paper showing through. Overlap the torn pieces.

You can also cut your mosaic pieces instead of tearing them. This is really better for making mosaic pictures, which take a little more time and care.

4. Make a Paper Picture

It is much easier to draw a shape and cut it out with scissors than to tear it, but if you are making a furry animal or a leafy tree you often get a better outline if you tear out your shapes.

Torn shapes are particularly good in tissue papers, as you can overlap the colours and get some good effects and movement.

Collect together:

Tissue Paper
Sheet of white paper for background
Paste
Brush.

Now begin:

Choose a simple shape and idea for your picture. Here is one called Bouncing Ball. Tear out all your tissue paper shapes before pasting them on to the white paper.

Now try an animal picture making the shapes out of news-papers.

Collect together:

Old newspapers
Black or brown background paper
Assorted coloured and textured papers from the paper box.

Now begin:

Decide which animals you are going to make and tear out the shapes in bright papers. It doesn't matter if they look odd; this should make them even more weird and amusing.

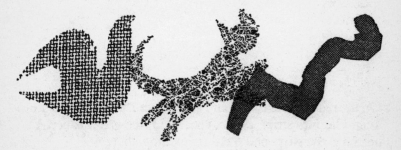

Paste a few torn newspaper mountains and trees, grasses and flowers to your background paper, now stick your animals over them in the foreground of the picture.

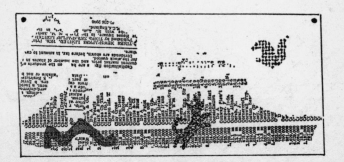

5. Make a Woven Paper Mat

Collect together:

Piece of card 6 ins. long and 6 ins. wide
Red paper ⎱
Green paper ⎰ – or any two other colours
Paste
Brush
Ruler
Scissors
Pencil.

Now begin:

On the red paper measure and rule 6 lines 1 in. wide and 7 ins. long. Cut into strips. Now repeat with the green paper. You need 6 green strips and 6 red strips altogether.

Paste the ends of the red strips side by side behind the top edge of the card. Paste the green strips side by side along the side edge of the card.

Now weave the first green strip UNDER AND OVER the red strips. Glue it down. When you have woven it right across, repeat with the second green strip but weave OVER AND UNDER. Carefully weave all the green strips through the red ones, making sure you get the right woven pattern as in Fig. 1. Be sure to glue down each strip when it has been woven.

Neaten any long edges.

6. Make a Paper Butterfly

Make sure that you use paper which is the same colour on both sides. *It should not be white on the back.*

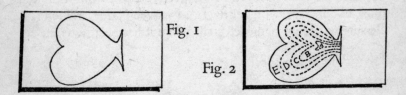

Fig. 1

Fig. 2

Collect together:

Sheet of white paper
2 sheets of coloured paper (with the colour on *both* sides)
Scissors
Paste
Pencil
Clothes peg.

Now begin:

Place the two sheets of coloured paper together.
Cut out two wings as in Fig. 1.

Lightly draw in the dotted lines on your cut out wings – see Fig. 2. Keeping the two wings firmly together, cut along the dotted lines. Now place all your cut out pieces before you and paste onto the white paper in this order – paste A in one colour opposite A in the other colour. Then follow with – B to B

C to C
D to D
and E to E.

You should now have a butterfly like this:

Cut out the butterfly and stick it on to the side edge of a clothes peg with strong glue. Now clip the butterfly on to your lamp-shade.

You can also make this butterfly in felts, and decorate it with sequins and beads.

7. Make a Line of Clowns

Collect together:

Sheet of white paper or card
Scissors
Coloured crayons
Pencil.

Now begin:

Make a fold in the paper 2 ins. from the edge. Crease the paper so that it folds forward. Make a second crease 2 ins. from the first but fold this so that it folds backward. Continue folding.

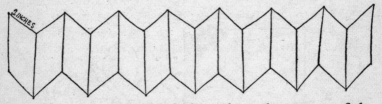

When you have finished folding, draw the picture of the clown on the top fold. Make sure the clown's elbows, knees and toes reach the edge of the paper. Cut round the figure.

Open out the paper and colour each clown differently.

8. Make a Paper Necklace

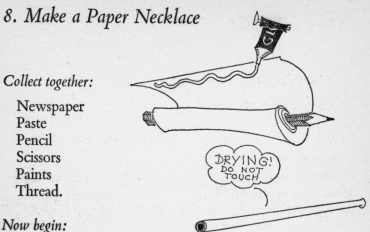

Collect together:

Newspaper
Paste
Pencil
Scissors
Paints
Thread.

Now begin:

Cut a piece of newspaper about 6 ins. × 6 ins. Roll it fairly loosely around the pencil and stick it together with glue. Slide the pencil out leaving a hollow paper tube. Leave until dry.

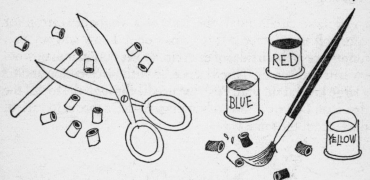

Cut the roll into $\frac{1}{2}$ in. beads with your scissors.
Paint each bead a bright colour and leave them to dry.
Go on working until you have about 60 beads.

Thread your beads. Knot the ends of the thread.

9. Make a Mobile

Collect together:

Stiff paper or card
Crayons
Wool
Strong glue
Sellotape
Black thread and needle
2 Pipecleaners – there is a special wire for mobiles which can be bought at art supply shops, but it is more expensive to use
Yoghourt carton.

Now begin:

Draw four circles using the base of a yoghourt carton (or your roll of sellotape if it is a small one). Draw and colour a funny face on both sides of each circle. Stick on strands of wool for hair and beards. Thread a needle with black cotton and tie a large knot at the end. Push the needle through the top of the first face. Leave the thread hanging. Attach a thread to each of the faces in the same way.

Twist the 2 pipecleaners together at the centre, then tie each face to a pipecleaner end so that it dangles on its thread. Make the faces hang at different heights. Tie a loop of thread round the centre of the pipecleaners and attach this to your lampshade or the ceiling.

You can make a fish mobile in the same way.

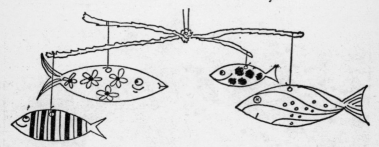

For Christmas you could make small paper snowflakes (see weather section) into a mobile decoration.

10. Make a Paper Collage

A paper collage is a picture made of different kinds and colours of paper. You can use paper collage instead of paints to make a frieze to decorate your bedroom wall. There are so many ideas for collage pictures that I am sure when you have made one you will want to make many more using different papers and shapes.

Collect together:

Your paper box
Scissors
Paste and brush
Sheet of paper for background.

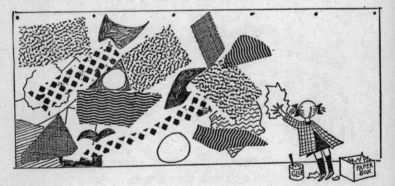

Now begin:

Either cut or tear your paper and paste each piece onto the background sheet. Use rough and smooth, thick and thin, bright and dull papers to give contrast and depth.

Leave a margin round your picture as a frame.

Remember to include shiny foil and toffee wrappers to add light to the picture.

11. Make Paper Flowers for the Papier Mâché Vase (No. 32)

Collect together:

Coloured tissue papers
6 Pipecleaners
Yellow and green paints.

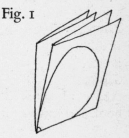

Fig. 1

Now begin:

Cut 6 squares of paper. Fold them in 4 like a handkerchief. Draw a petal shape on the folded paper as in Fig. 1. Cut round this shape.

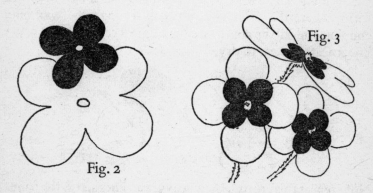

Fig. 2

Fig. 3

Cut 6 smaller squares. Fold and cut them in the same way. Place 1 small flower on top of each large flower. (Fig. 2.)

Dip the tips of 6 pipecleaners in yellow paint. Push 1 yellow tip through 2 of the petals then coil it round to stop the petals falling off (Fig. 3). Repeat for other 5 pipecleaner stalks. Paint the rest of the pipecleaner green.

12. Make a Cover for Your Scrapbook

Collect together:

Candles
Paints
Brushes
Paste
Scissors
A sheet of coloured paper large enough to cover the scrapbook and leave a margin all round.

Now begin:

Use a candle to make wavy patterns across the paper, pressing down well so as to leave a trail of wax. Paint across the entire paper, using only a little paint on your brush. A *wax resist* will form, where the paint will not soak through the wax lines and you will still be able to see the original colour of the paper underneath. Leave to dry.

Now repeat this creating new wavy wax lines across the paint. When a second layer of paint in a different colour is spread over the paper a further wax resist will show through and part of your first layer of paint will be preserved.

There are many different ways of making a wax resist, using paper or material. Simply remember that where a wax pattern has been drawn paint will not be absorbed, and you should get some interesting effects.

Spread paste all over the back of your cover. Place the open scrapbook in the centre of the sheet. Close the book carefully smoothing out any creases in the cover.

Open out the book again at the front and fold the margins in so that the scrapbook has a neat edge.

Neaten these margins as below.

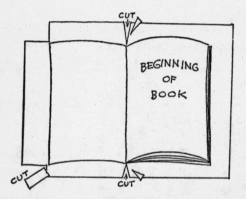

Now do the same at the back.

13. Make Stained-glass Windows

Collect together:
Coloured tissue or cellophane papers
Scissors
Sheet of black paper
Paste.

Now begin:
Cut the black paper into a church-window shape.

Cut shapes out of the black paper as shown. Now paste different coloured scraps of tissue over the holes.

Turn the window back to the other side so that no pasting shows. If you attach it to a window, the light will shine through the coloured tissue paper like a real stained-glass window.

14. Make a Zig-Zag Book

Take:
A long strip
   of card.

Now begin:

Fold the card in half, then in half again. Now re-fold so that the book stands up on its own in a zig-zag. Use this book as a scrapbook or for your poem collection.

15. Make Tangrams

This is an old Chinese puzzle that is great fun.

Collect together:

White paper
Scissors
Coloured crayons
Tracing paper.

Now begin:

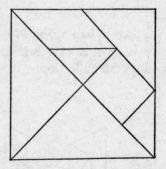

Trace this pattern *exactly* onto the white paper. Colour each shape a different colour and cut them out. Make pictures and patterns using these shapes, like the one below.

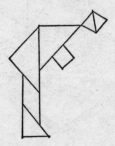

16. Make Tissue Pom-poms

Collect together:

Scissors
Needle and thread
2 different-coloured sheets of tissue paper
Yoghourt carton.

Now begin:

Cut 8 circles of tissue paper tracing round the base of a yog-hourt carton. Fold each circle in half, then in quarters.

Thread your needle and tie a large knot in the end. Thread each folded circle through the corner onto your cotton, alternating the colours. Put two stitches through the final one to secure the thread.

Carefully pull each folded circle open.

Hang from the ceiling or from the light.

17. Make Coin Pictures

Collect together:

Different-sized coins
Paper
Pencil
Coloured crayons.

Now begin:

Draw round the coins to make patterns, people, flowers, animals – anything else you can think of. Colour them neatly.

18. Make a Paper Lantern

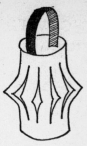

Collect together:

Paste
Scissors
Sheet of paper.

Now begin:

Cut an oblong of paper about 9 ins. long and 6 ins. wide. Fold it in half, then snip strips upwards from the fold. Do not cut right across the folded paper.

Open out the paper and, bending it round, paste one edge over the other.

Cut a small strip of paper and paste across the top to act as a handle loop.

Decorate your lantern with paints or sticky papers.

You can also use the lantern like a hanging basket and fill it with tissue paper pom-poms made in bright colours (see No. 16).

MAKING WITH MATERIAL

Before you start you should collect together as many scraps of material, wool and ribbons as you can. Also make sure you have a needle which you can thread yourself, sewing cotton and a pair of scissors you find easy to use.

You will probably make lots of mess, so put some newspaper over the table or floor before you begin.

When sewing begin by tying a small knot in your thread and finish off securely with two stitches one over the other.

19. Make a String-holder Cat

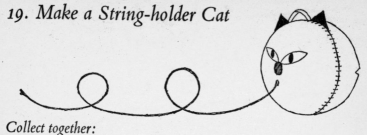

Collect together:

Felt or stiff fabric
A saucer
Coloured scraps of fabric
A needle and cotton
4 broom bristles

A small coin
Scissors
Strong glue
Pencil
A ball of string
Small length of ribbon.

Now begin:

Place the saucer upside down on the felt and draw round it. Cut out the circle, then cut out another exactly the same. Cut a small hole in the first circle and a long slit in the second. (Fig. 1.)

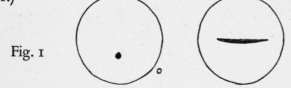

Fig. 1

Using different fabrics cut out two eyes and a nose the size of a small coin and glue them onto the face (Fig. 2). Cut out two ears and glue them between the two circles. Fold a small piece of ribbon and glue it between the ears (Fig. 2).

Fig. 2

Now oversew the circles together neatly all the way round taking care to leave the ears and loop sticking up.

Push the four bristles through the cheeks for whiskers.

The ball of string goes through the slit at the back and the end is pulled through the hole in the front. Now you have a string holder.

20. Make a Pencil Cover

Collect together:

A pencil	Cotton wool
Scissors	Scraps of material
Felt	Strong glue
A ruler	An egg cup.

Fig. 1

Now begin:

Cut a piece of felt 7 ins. long and 1½ ins. wide. Spread a little glue down one of the long edges then carefully fold it round your pencil. Glue it to the other side so that you have a long felt pipe which slides easily off your pencil. Close the pipe with strong glue at one end. Now cut two circles the size of the top of an egg cup. Glue these together with a little cotton wool stuck in between the circles at the top to make hair (Fig. 1). Cut out and glue on eyes, ears and a mouth as in the diagram. Glue the head to the closed end of the felt pipe. Keep your favourite pencil safe in its new cover.

21. Make a Patterned Knick-knack Holder

Here is a new home for your toothbrush, or your comb or even your pencils and pens.

Collect together:

A clean yoghourt carton
Scraps of fabric
A 9-inch length of braid or ribbon
Scissors
Strong glue.

Now begin:

Cut out circles and squares from different coloured scraps of material and stick them onto the outside of the yoghourt carton until it is completely covered – and very colourful.

Glue the braid right round the top of the carton to hide the rim.

What a splendid holder! You could do this with coloured paper too.

22. Make a Puffin Book Cover

Here is a cover to slip on to whichever Puffin you are reading at the moment. This will protect it from stains or puppy teeth.

PUFFIN BOOK

Fig. 1

Collect together:

Stiff material
Pencil
Scissors
Pins
Needle
Cotton

Scraps of felt
Strong glue
Ruler.

Now begin:

Measure a piece of material 15 ins. long and $8\frac{1}{2}$ ins. wide, and cut it out. Fold in a 2 ins. strip at each end (Fig. 1). Pin the folds at the top and the bottom (Fig. 1). Neatly oversew the edges so that they are firm. (You may glue them if you prefer.)

Now fold your cover as it will slip onto the book, and decorate the front with interesting patterns cut from scraps of felt and glued on.

Fig. 2

23. Make a Fabric Collage

A fabric collage is a picture made up of pieces of fabric, embroidery, beads, buttons, lace, etc., in fact anything you have in your fabric scrapbag.

You can also make a paper collage (No. 10).

Collect together:

> Strong glue
> Scissors
> Assorted fabrics
> Background fabric, at least 12 ins. × 12 ins.

Now begin:

Make your collage anything you like; an animal, flowers or leaves, a bird, or just a pattern. (If you like, draw your picture on paper first, then you will have a guide to follow.)

Simply cut out your fabric pieces and stick them onto the background fabric. Staple or sew the collage onto a firm piece of card, leaving a small margin of card showing all round as a mount.

Collages also look their best when used as a cushion cover. Cut a second piece of fabric the same size as your collage to make the back of the cover.

Turn the two right sides to face each other and sew neatly round three of the edges. Use a small running stitch $\frac{1}{2}$ in. in from the edge of the fabric. Turn your cushion cover to the right sides and stuff with an old cushion, a bag of foam, or a small pillow.

Turn the edges of the fourth side neatly in and oversew to close up the cushion cover.

A simple pattern using overlapping shapes.

Remember that the more different the kinds of fabric you use, and the more care you take in choosing your colours, the better your collage will be. Overlap delicate fabrics onto heavy ones to make shadows.

24. Making your Mark

Here's how to embroider your name on things which you want to make especially yours, like a towel, an apron or a shoe bag.

Collect together:

Pencil	Towel	Needle
	Silk	Scissors.

Now begin:

Write your name in joined-up writing across the material. Sew over your name in running stitch. Then weave in and out of the stitches in a different colour.

25. Make a Peg Doll

You will need an old-fashioned peg with a round knob at the end. These can be bought at hardware stores but many mothers or grandmothers will have one like this in their peg bags.

Collect together:

  1 round-headed peg
  Scraps of fabric, sequins, beads
  Strong glue
  Needle, cotton, scissors
  Wool scraps
  2 pipe cleaners
  Pink paint
  Black felt pen.

Now begin:

First paint the head of the peg pink. Let it dry and then draw a face on it in black felt pen.

Fold the pipecleaner in two and crease it firmly. Thread the pipecleaner between the prongs of the peg, so the fold fits neatly under the round head. Raise the two ends of the pipe-cleaner so they are the same length above the head, and wrap the second pipe cleaner tightly round to keep them in place.

Now bend the pipecleaner ends down again to form arms.

The pipecleaner wrapped round as the body will give you a firm base to which you can attach a gathered skirt and a lace bodice. Dress your doll in a long gown, decorated with lace and sequins. Drape flowing sleeves over the pipecleaner arms. These can be stuck on with strong glue. Cut lengths of wool and glue them to the crown of the head. Cut a circular hat in felt and stick a small feather through it.

26. Make a Frog Bean-Bag

Collect together:

Material
Scissors
Felt scraps
Strong glue
Needle and cotton
Pins
Packet of dried peas, or beans.

Now begin:

Cut two frog shapes out of your material. Choose a different colour for each shape.

Pin the shapes together leaving a small gap unpinned at the head. Sew neatly round the frog in running stitch keeping about $\frac{1}{2}$ inch in from the edge. Do not sew across the gap. Turn inside out and fill with dried peas or beans.

Oversew the gap at the edge, first turning the raw edges inside.

Cut out 2 large eyes and glue on top of the head.

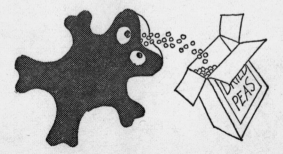

27. *Make a Draught-stopper Snake*

Collect together:

A length of hessian a little longer than the width of your door and 18 ins. wide
Needle
Thread
Scraps of material
2 buttons
Scissors
Strong glue
Rags for stuffing.

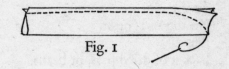

Fig. 1

Now begin:

Fold your material in half lengthwise and sew neatly along the edges until you are 6 ins. from the end. Then sew tapering inwards to the fold to make a rounded point (see Fig. 1).

Trim the edges with scissors.

Turn your snake's body inside out and stuff with any rags you can find. Make running stitches round the open end and gather. Fasten off (see Fig. 2).

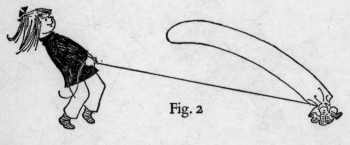

Fig. 2

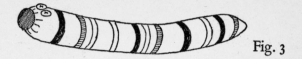

Fig. 3

Cut narrow strips of different-coloured material and glue them in bands round the snake's body. Cut a large circle and, pressing the gathered opening down flat, glue or sew the circle over the gathered hole so as to cover the frayed edges.

Sew two buttons above the circle for eyes (see Fig. 3).

28. Make a Pin-cushion

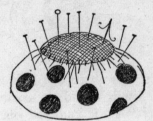

Collect together:

Tea plate
Pencil
Needle
Cotton
Material
Kapok.

Now begin:

Draw a circle round the base of the tea plate on the piece of material. Cut it out. Thread the needle with cotton and knot it at the end. Sew with small running stitches right round the edge of the circle (Fig. 1). Pull this thread and gather the stitches tightly (Fig. 2). The round cushion you have made must now be stuffed tightly with kapok, before you fasten off your thread securely.

Cut a small circle of material (or a square) large enough to cover the gathering thread, and oversew or glue it neatly over the top (Fig. 3).

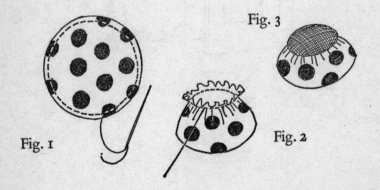

Fig. 3

Fig. 1

Fig. 2

29. Make a Strap Purse

Collect together:

A piece of felt 9 ins. × 5 ins.
Needle and cotton
Scissors
Length of cord
Pins.

Now begin:

Fold the piece of material in half. Pin the side edges together and oversew neatly (see Fig. 1).

Fig. 1   Fig. 2

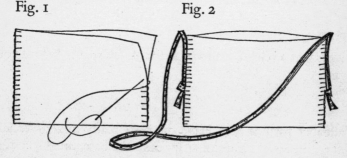

Knot the cord at each end to stop it fraying. Then sew it to each oversewn edge as in Fig. 2.

Keep your handkerchief or purse in this strap holder. To make it really secure either sew poppers along the top inside edges; or sew a loop of cord to the centre top of one side and sew a button the size of the loop just below the centre top of the other side. The loop will bend over the button to close the gap firmly (Fig. 3).

Fig. 3

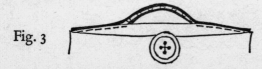

MAKE WITH PAPIER MÂCHÉ

Papier mâché is French for pulped paper, and this explains exactly what you will be using. The torn shreds of paper are soaked in paste and either placed over a shape to form a hard crust when dry, or modelled into different shapes in the same way that you use plasticine. Both methods are used in this section, but the essential rule for both is to let your papier mâché dry firmly before beginning the next stage.

Base

Papier mâché tends to stick firmly to whatever base you are using, so always cover the base with a thick layer of Vaseline first to prevent this.

Paper

Always tear a pile of scraps or strips of newspaper before you begin.

Paste

Wallpaper paste is best. Have the paste ready mixed. When pasting, place the scraps or strips onto the base, one layer at a time, and leave each until it is completely dry.

Drying

5–6 layers of papier mâché make a solid frame. Leave your model overnight in the airing cupboard or near a radiator to make it dry quicker.

30. Make an Owl

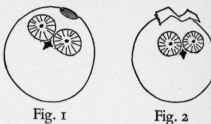

Fig. 1   Fig. 2

Collect together:

Balloon
Newspaper
Thin paste (flour or wallpaper paste)
Paints and a brush
Dried peas
Small paper handkerchief.

Now begin:

Blow up the balloon to the size you want and knot the end. Smear the balloon lightly with Vaseline then cover it with papier mâché as described on the previous page. Leave the knot clear.

When the papier mâché is completely dry burst the balloon and pull it loose.

Fill the body with enough dried peas to keep it standing upright.

Now draw the owl's face as in Fig. 1, and paint him. Don't forget the back.

Fold the paper handkerchief in two and glue it over the hole at the top to make his ears (Fig. 2).

31. You Can Also Make a Pirate, or a Father Christmas

Use the same method as for an owl, but draw on the different lines for painting the face. Father Christmas looks fine with cotton wool stuck round his chin and a large red paper napkin knotted over his head. Show a little more cotton wool under his cap for snowy white hair.

The pirate must look villainous and black lengths of wool stuck under his cap can make his dark, lank hair. Sew a brass curtain ring onto his head to make the golden ring looped in one ear.

32. Make a Vase for Paper Flowers

To make the flowers – see Making Paper Flowers, No. 11.

Collect together:

Newspaper
Thin paste
Empty lemonade bottle
Brush
Paints
Scissors.

Now begin:

Smear the lower half of the bottle with Vaseline, then cover with papier mâché as described.

When dry gently remove the bottle. Trim the rim of the vase, then paint it in a pretty colour or pattern so that no newspaper shows through.

Do remember this vase is for paper flowers only and WILL NOT hold water.

33. Make a Crocodile

Collect together:

Newspaper
Thin paste
Paints
Brush
String
Large-eyed needle.

Now begin:

Make several round papier mâché balls of different sizes –
large, medium and small – as below. Then make one long
one, like a sausage, for the head and flatten half of it. Leave
them until they are quite dry. Paint the balls. Paint eyes above
the flattened snout.

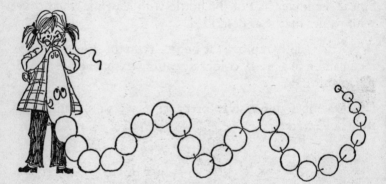

Thread a needle with string and tie a knot in the end. Thread
the smallest ball on the string, then the next smallest, and so
on, until you get to the large one which is the snout. Tie a
knot in the string and cut off.

34. Make a Moon Base for a Rocket

You know that the surface of the Moon is covered with craters and rocks, and that it is a grey, bleak place, so paint your model in dull, cold colours.

Collect together:

Toilet roll holders   Tin foil
Egg shells   Paste
Strong glue   Large sheet of thick card
Egg boxes   Paints.
Scissors

Now begin:

Paint the sheet of card grey, black and white. Smear the colours for the right shadowy effect. When dry spread paste over the model and stick small pieces of eggshell here and there. Spot these with grey paint. Tear off individual egg cups from the egg boxes and glue them on as humps and holes. Add rings of cardboard roll for craters. Pile egg shell round the base to make the steep slopes. Paste pieces of tin foil inside the craters.

Glue or just place a rocket on the Moon (see No. 61).

MAKING A WEATHER RECORD

Here's a chance to be a weather detective.

How well can you watch the weather, watch *how* it changes, and watch *when* it changes, and then put all these discoveries onto paper as a Weather Chart, or as a pattern or even as a poem?

35. Make a Weather Chart

Collect together:

Large sheet of white card or stiff paper
Pencil   Ruler   Crayons.

Now begin:

Rule your sheet into large squares. If you are going to watch the weather for one week, morning and afternoon, you will need 14 squares as below.

	SUN	MON	TUES	WED	THURS	FRI	SAT
A.M.							

	SUN	MON	TUES	WED	THURS	FRI	SAT
P.M.							

If you are watching for a month and will be recording once a day, make a chart like this:

1	2	3	4	5	6	7
8	9	10	11	12	13	14
15	16	17	18	19	20	21
22	23	24	25	26	27	28
29	30	31				

Here are weather symbols:

Rain

Snow

Sunshine

Windy

Foggy or Misty

Cloudy

Draw in the correct symbols for each day's weather every day.

36. Make a Wind Chart

Keep a record of the direction in which the wind blows each day.

Collect together:

Large sheet of white card
Pencil
Compass
Handkerchief.

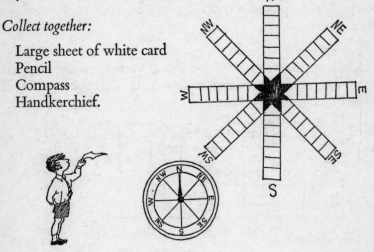

Now begin:

If you plan to record for a week, make a chart like this with spaces to record the wind for seven days, and mark on the points of the compass as shown. Colour the centre black.

Use your compass the first day to show you which direction is north, and turn your chart north in the same direction. Then hold up a handkerchief, watch the cock on a weather vane, or watch smoke from a chimney to decide where the wind is blowing from.

Each day colour in a square on the appropriate arm of your chart to mark the direction of the wind. On the first day you should colour in the correct square 1, on the second day the correct square 2, and so on.

37. Make Snowflake Patterns

If you looked at a snowflake under a microscope you would see a beautiful pattern. It is very delicate and light. Can you make one in paper? It would be a good way of decorating your weather charts.

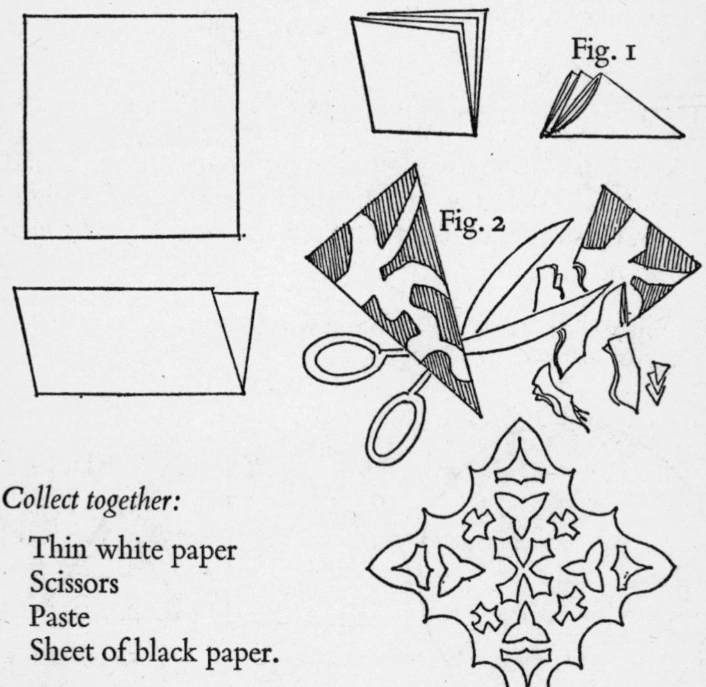

Fig. 1

Fig. 2

Collect together:

Thin white paper
Scissors
Paste
Sheet of black paper.

Now begin:

Cut a square of white paper about the size of a handkerchief. Fold it in half, and then into quarters. Fold once again (Fig. 1). Draw loops on this folded paper as in Fig. 2. Cut out the shaded areas. Open out your snowflake.

Cut more, making them smaller and smaller, and then stick them onto the black paper.

38. Make More Snowflakes

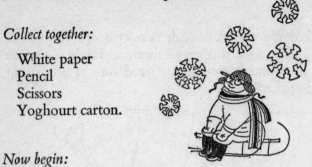

Collect together:

White paper
Pencil
Scissors
Yoghourt carton.

Now begin:

On your paper draw a circle round the yoghourt carton and cut it out. Fold the circle in half, then in quarters and eighths. Shade in the area as in Fig. 2. Cut out this shaded area. Open up your snowflake.

Stick onto black paper or onto the window during winter for the best effect.

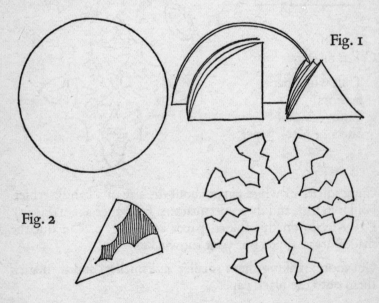

Fig. 1

Fig. 2

39. Make Frost Patterns

Collect together:

White poster paint
Brush
Thin paste
Sheet of dark coloured card.

Now begin:

Mix a little paste with the white paint. Stir well. Brush this mixture quite thickly all over the coloured card.

With your nails or finger tips make patterns in the white paste. Keep your fingers tightly together and turn and twist them. Make loops and swirls and fern shapes.

40. Make a Cloud Chart

If you have enjoyed recording weather changes here is one last record to make for your collection. It is a Cloud Chart, but first you must learn to recognize different cloud shapes.

1	2	3	4	5	6	7
8	9	10	11	12	13	14
15	16	17	18	19	20	21
22	23	24	25	26	27	28
29	30	31				

Your Cloud Chart looks like the Weather Chart (No 35). Using the shapes below as symbols, keep a daily record of clouds you see in the sky.

Thin wispy clouds high in the sky on a fine day.

White, fluffy cotton-wool clouds seen on sunny days. These sometimes bring showers.

A grey sheet of cloud covering the sky on dull, windless days. They often mean drizzle.

High piles of grey clouds usually mean rain and wind.

Heavy black and grey clouds bringing heavy rain and sometimes thunderstorms.

41. Weather Poetry

I'm sure after all the weather watching and recording you have done you are now real experts in noticing how the weather changes everything, even how we feel ourselves.

Have you noticed how different the garden looks in the sunshine and in the rain?

Why not try to make a different sort of record this time, a personal one which tells how you feel about the weather.

Take a good look outside first and think of some words which describe what you can see. These might help if it's sunny:

Golden; shady; shining; bright; colourful.

Write your sunshine words in the shape of a big, round sun.

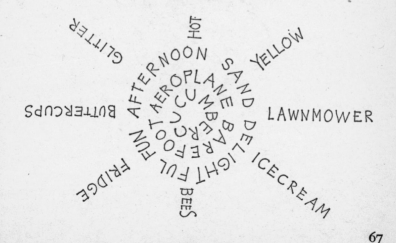

And a rainbow in rainbow words?

ULTRAMARINE FORTUNE ORANGE
UP GREEN YELLOW DOWN
SPECTRUM RAINDROPS

Then try more difficult shapes: stars, umbrellas, snowflakes, lightning, and fireworks.

When you have a collection of simple poems, go on and try more difficult things.

42. Make a Seaside Scrapbook

Very likely you enjoy a long holiday at the seaside each summer. This year why not keep a holiday record to cheer you through the cold wintry months that follow, and keep happy memories alive?

Make a scrapbook (as in No. 1).

Cover the outer sheets with drawings of you swimming in the sea, building sandcastles, climbing rocks or shrimping. Print neatly on the cover –

MY HOLIDAY IN –

and put the dates you were there below it.

Fill your scrapbook with:

(a) an account of places and things you passed on the journey
(b) snapshots
(c) a short day-by-day account of your activities
(d) postcards
(e) dried seaweed
(f) drawings of shells, fish, etc.
(g) all kinds of other information
– and don't forget a weather and wind chart.

43. Make a Weather Folder

Have you managed all this weather work?

Why not make a folder out of thin card to hold all your weather information? You may find you can add to it later on, or use it in project work at school.

Simply fold a large sheet of card in three as shown in the diagram and decorate the front with different kinds of weather symbols or snowflake patterns. Print WEATHER neatly on the front. (Make sure the folder is big enough to hold all your charts.)

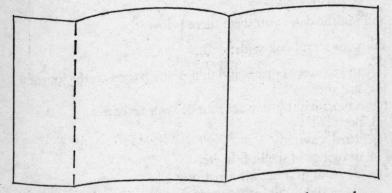

The fold section can be stitched or glued back so that you have an additional pocket into which information can be tucked.

44. Make an Autumn Tree

Leaves turn such beautiful colours in autumn – here is a way of mounting them so that all the colours tone together.

Collect together:

Large sheet of white paper or newspaper
Brown paint
Brush
As many leaves of different sizes, shapes and colours as you can find
Strong glue.

Now begin:

Paint a broad tree trunk and branches in brown paint on the sheet of paper. When completely dry glue different leaves over the branches.

Pin this autumn picture on the wall.

MAKING WITH WOOL

Collect a wool bag as you did with material and paper. Even small lengths will come in useful.

45. *Make a Wool Picture*

Collect together:

Strong glue
Scissors
Strong paper
Odd balls of coloured wool
Pencil.

Now begin:

Draw a picture on the paper. Choose large, bold flowers, or animals or any easy shape. Cut lengths of wool to the right length and stick them in place. In other places glue the wool down in circles or spirals.

Make a simple pattern if you want something easier and quicker to make.

46. Make a Woolly Dormouse

Collect together:

Odd balls of wool
Milk bottle or yoghourt carton
Scissors
Cardboard
A small coin
Short length of thick string.

Now begin:

Draw 2 circles on the cardboard using the bottom of the yoghourt carton or the milk bottle. Cut them out. Cut out a smaller circle the size of a small coin from the centre of each (Fig. 1).

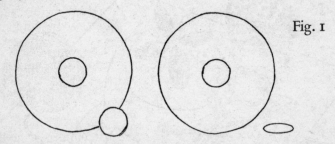

Fig. 1

Put the two circles together and wind the wool round and round, joining on a fresh colour whenever you want to.

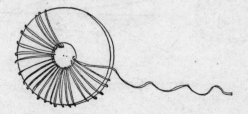

Continue until it is really difficult to push the wool through the centre hole. You might even need a thick needle to help you pull the last few lengths through.

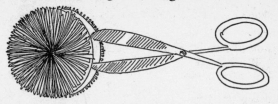

Now cut round the edge of the wool circles between the cardboard edges. When all the strands are cut, wind a length of wool tightly between the cardboard circles, so that the wool is held tightly at the centre. Cut away the cardboard circles and fluff out the wool. You may need to trim the ends a bit to make the pompom even.

Cut out small felt shapes for the eyes and ears and stick them on to the ball to make the dormouse – fast asleep.

For his tail

Tie a length of thick string to the wool that holds the centre, knot it near the end then fray the end.

Make 2 tiny pom-poms for a baby friend or your cat to play with. Or make a really large dormouse, using saucer-sized circles, to sit on your bed.

47. Make Dougall

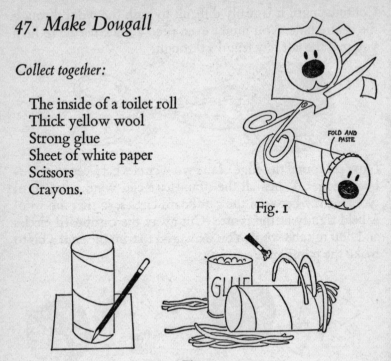

Fig. 1

Collect together:

The inside of a toilet roll
Thick yellow wool
Strong glue
Sheet of white paper
Scissors
Crayons.

Fig. 2

Now begin:

Place the roll upright on the paper and draw around it. Draw in a face as on Fig. 1. Cut round the circle about 1 in. outside the pencil circle. Paste this over the hole as in Fig. 2.

Cut a pile of wool lengths 5 ins. long. Begin at the face and glue on the wool as in Fig. 3 to make a shaggy fringe round the face. Cover the space at the back completely. Glue the rest of the wool across the roll so that it hangs down on each side. Glue on thickly so that no cardboard roll shows through.

Fig. 3

MAKING PATTERNS

Patterns are great fun to make. You can squirl, squiggle, twirl and twiddle. You can make squares or circles, use all kinds of pattern blocks, use many colours or just two. Here are just a few ideas. You will think of others, I'm sure.

48. Make a Wax Scratch

Collect together:

Wax crayons including black
Scissors
Sheet of paper.

Now begin:

Mark off the paper into squares and colour them different colours, *except* black.

Now crayon in black over all the other coloured squares.

With the scissor points, gently scratch circular patterns or any other patterns across the sheet, so that the black wax is scraped off to leave different colours showing through.

49. Make a Mirror Pattern

Collect together:

Coloured paints
Brush
Sheet of paper.

Now begin:

Fold the sheet of paper in half and open it out again.

Using just two colours paint thickly on one half of the paper only. Then, while the paint is still wet, fold the painted half and the plain half of the paper together again. Press firmly, then open the paper out to see your mirror pattern.

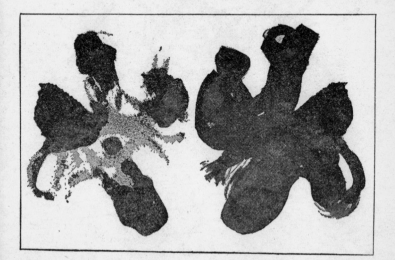

50. *Make Drip Patterns*

Collect together:

Paint, mixed fairly thickly
Thin paint brushes
Sheet of paper.

Now begin:

Drip dots of different-coloured paints all over the paper then blow *gently* across the sheet to smudge them. Choose two or three colours that tone well together.

51. Make Dribble Patterns

Collect together:

Paint, mixed fairly thickly
Thin paint brushes
Sheet of paper.

Now begin:

Drop one colour of paint thickly across the centre of the paper. Hold the paper upright and let the paint dribble downwards. Then turn it upside down and let paint dribble back to other edge of paper.

Drop a second layer of different coloured paint across the centre line and repeat the dribble process.

52. Make Animal Silhouettes

Collect together:

Scissors
Black paper
Large sheet of white paper
Chalk
Paste and brush.

Now begin:

Choose your favourite animals. Think of some you have seen in a zoo, or at the circus. Draw them on the black paper with chalk, then cut them out carefully and paste them onto the large white sheet.

Arrange them in a zoo (or a circus) scene, drawing railings and pools, trees and visitors around them.

53. Make a Finger Pattern

Collect together:

    Paints
    Thin paste
    Sheet of white paper
    Paintbrush
    Old spoon.

Now begin:

Mix a jar of thick paint and add to it a quarter of a jar of paste mix. Stir well. Pour a little of the paint/paste mix onto the centre of the paper then spread it evenly all over the paper with the brush.

Now with your first three fingers firmly together make finger patterns across the paper. You can make exciting squiggles and swirls.

Then leave to dry.

54. Make a Comb Pattern

Collect together:

Paints	Old comb
Paste	Paintbrush
Paper	Old spoon.

Now begin:

Do the same as you did for finger painting (No. 53), except this time you make the patterns with the comb instead of your fingers.

55. Make a Hand Pattern

Collect together:

Coloured paints
Brushes
Large sheet of white paper.

Now begin:

Here is a really messy pattern session – after which you will need a good scrub.

Paint your left hand palm with a brightly coloured paint (thickly mixed powder paint is best) then press it down firmly on the sheet of paper. Don't let your hand slip or you will blur the print. Then press more hand prints over the paper facing different ways, using other colours.

When you have finished a sheet of successful prints, start again and make a more formal hand pattern. Place your first print in the top left corner with fingers at the top. Turn the paper and place the next print upside down beside the first. Continue with this alternating pattern.

56. Make an Alphabet Montage

Collect together:

> Magazines
> Scissors
> Paste
> Sheet of paper.

Now begin:

Cut out letters, large and small, coloured, white and black, capital and italic. Arrange them haphazardly over the sheet of paper and paste them down. Put some letters upside down. Occasionally paste in a complete word – choose humorous ones.

57. Make a Face Montage

Collect together:

Magazines
Scissors
Paste
Sheet of paper.

Now begin:

Go through some old magazines and cut out as many different eyes, ears, noses and mouths as you can find. Glue them all over the paper to make a mixed collection of features.

MAKING DO WITH ODDS AND ENDS

There are all sorts of odds and ends around the house that can be used to make small toys. If you can collect some of these, in a large Odds and Ends Box, you will then be ready to start making things.

    Cotton reels
    Seeds
    Card
    Egg boxes
    Toilet rolls
    Washing-up liquid cartons
    Egg shells

58. Make a Cotton-reel Snake

Collect together:

As many empty cotton reels as you can find
Thin string
A button
Coloured paints
Brushes.

Fig. 1

Now begin:

Paint each cotton reel a different colour and leave them to dry.
Choose one cotton reel for the head. Paint the head as in Fig. 1
with two evil-looking eyes.

Tie a large knot in the string then thread it through all the
cotton reels. Leave 2 ins. of string poking from the head and
cut the string off. Divide the string in two by untwisting it.
Poke each end through a hole in the button. Knot twice and
leave as the tongue.

59. Make Cotton-reel Animals

Collect together:

A cotton reel
Scissors
Paints
Strong glue
Pencil
Cotton
Card, stiff and white.

Now begin:

Take 2 pieces of stiff white card. Draw round the cotton reel in the centre of each, then sketch in the front and back body shapes of your chosen animal, for instance a cat, round the circles. Cut out each shape. Paint them on both sides, not forgetting to give the cat eyes, a mouth and whiskers, but not on the back of his head.

Paint the cotton reel all over to match the colour of the card shapes.

Glue front shape of cat to front of cotton reel and back shape of cat to back of cotton reel.

Make sure the feet are level so that he stands up.

Make all sorts of different animals in the same way.

60. Make a Wall Plaque

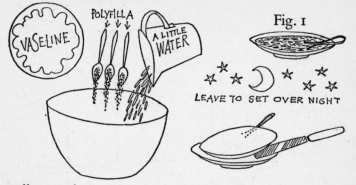

Fig. 1

LEAVE TO SET OVER NIGHT

Collect together:

Polyfilla	Small length of string or ribbon
Basin	Picture or photograph
Old spoon	Blunt knife
Old saucer	Paste.
Vaseline	

Now begin:

Smear the inside of the saucer thickly with Vaseline.

Mix half a basin of Polyfilla (about 3 tablespoons) with a little water until stiff. Pour slowly into the saucer until it is completely full. Level off the top with the smooth side of the spoon. Loop a small piece of string and press it well into the Polyfilla at the edge of the saucer (see Fig. 1).

Leave the Polyfilla to set overnight. When it is completely set tap the saucer gently to loosen the cast and ease it out of the saucer with a blunt knife. Cut a photograph of yourself or any picture to fit the circle in the centre of the plaque. Paste this on and hang the plaque on your wall.

61. Make a Rocket

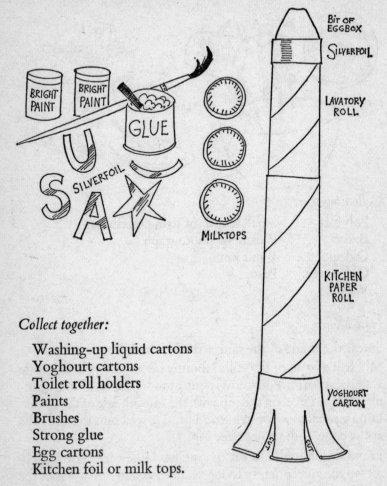

BIT OF EGGBOX

SILVERFOIL

LAVATORY ROLL

KITCHEN PAPER ROLL

YOGHOURT CARTON

CUT

CUT

Collect together:

Washing-up liquid cartons
Yoghourt cartons
Toilet roll holders
Paints
Brushes
Strong glue
Egg cartons
Kitchen foil or milk tops.

Now begin:

According to the size of your different cartons, fit them together to make the sections of the rocket. See diagram.

Paint your model with thick, bright paint and after it is dry decorate it with signs and symbols in silver foil.

62. Make an Egg-shell Picture

Collect together:

    Paste and a brush
    Sheet of coloured card
    Crushed egg shells
    Pencil.

Now begin:

Draw a large fish on the coloured card. Glue fragments of egg shell onto the fish to make a pattern of scales.

63. Make a Seed Mat

Collect together:

Polyfilla
Water
Basin, old spoon or stick
Lid from cocoa or other shallow tin
Dried peas, lentils, beans, macaroni, rice, etc.

Now begin:

Mix a small quantity of Polyfilla and water to a very stiff paste in the basin. Spoon it gently into the cocoa-tin lid, and smooth it evenly across.

Select your dried seeds, and place them in the wet Polyfilla one by one to make a star or flower pattern. Use different-coloured seeds.

64. Make a Salt Figure

Collect together:

Block of salt
Blunt kitchen knife
Newspaper.

Now begin:

Spread out a newspaper and put the salt block on it. Choose an animal figure to carve. Now scrape away with the knife, cutting and carving until you have your animal. Make your animal lie down or sit up as salt legs will often crumble away.

65. Make a Melon-seed Necklace

If you have melon to eat one day ask your mother to save the seeds for you.

Collect together:

Melon seeds, well washed and dried
Needle
Strong thread, long enough for a necklace
Jar of paint.

Now begin:

Tie a large knot at the end of the thread before you start to thread the melon seeds. You can string them easily if you push the needle through the end of the seed. Thread as many melon seeds as you can. Knot the remaining thread through the first seed you sewed and fasten off.

Dip the necklace into the pot of paint and hang it up to dry.

MAKE A PRINT

Printing is great fun and you can use many different types of blocks to make your pattern. A block can be made by cutting potatoes and carrots, or by glueing string.

Print a large sheet with repeating patterns for the best effects, and use your printed sheet to cover your books or for the outside of a scrapbook.

Polish your cover with a little colourless wax polish on a duster to seal the paint colours and make it water-, dust- and spill-proof.

66. Make a Potato Print

Collect together:

A potato
Knife
Paints – 2 colours
Brush
Sheet of white paper.

Now begin:

Cut the potato in half. Cut out jagged or curved shapes on the flat side of one half of the potato. Remember that the pattern you will print is left by the raised bits of the potato, not the shapes you cut away (see Fig. 1). Then cut a different pattern on the other half-potato.

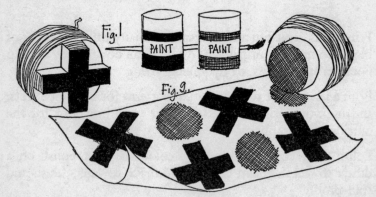

Paint the raised bits of one potato half with one colour and press it down well into the top corner of the sheet. Paint the second potato-half with the other colour and print beside the first. Repeat the prints as in Fig. 2 until the entire sheet is patterned.

Use a carrot if you do not have a potato.

67. Make a String Print

Collect together:

A square of very stiff cardboard, lino, or wood
Thick string
Scissors
Strong glue
Paints
Brush
Sheet of white paper.

Now begin:

Decide whether you are going to print in a special shape or just in patterns (see Fig. 1).

Cut a length of string about two feet long. Glue one end of it to the square of cardboard, or whatever you are using, putting just a dab of glue on the string. Slowly stick the rest of the string onto the board, coiling it as you go into a circle pattern or any other shape. This is your string print block. By covering it all over with a little paint and pressing it upside down onto the sheet of paper you will make a coloured string print. Repeat the print for a completely patterned paper.

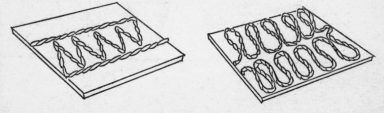

68. Make a Carrot Print

Collect together:

Paints
Brushes
Sheet of white paper
Kitchen knife
Carrot.

Now begin:

Cut circular pieces of carrot of all sizes. Cut pieces out of the carrots for a more interesting print.

Print as for the potato print. With the largest circles print an alternating pattern, leaving spaces for smaller carrot prints.

Use different-coloured paints and long strips of carrot to print the bar pattern (see Fig. 1).

Fig. 1

69. Make a Coin Rubbing

Collect together:

Different sized and shaped coins (use foreign ones if you have them)
Sheet of thin white paper such as typewriting paper
Black wax crayon.

Now begin:

Place the sheet of paper over a coin and rub lightly over it with your wax crayon. The rubbing should bring out an exact copy of the pattern on the coin. Rub other coins onto the sheet in the same way.

70. Make Leaf Prints

Collect together:

Thick paints
Brushes
White paper
Newspaper
Different leaves.

Now begin:

Take one leaf and paint lightly over the side on which the veins stick up. Place it carefully paint side down on the white paper then put the newspaper carefully over the leaf. Rub slowly but firmly over the newspaper, then remove both newspaper and leaf carefully and see your outlined leaf.

Repeat with leaves of all shapes and sizes, and with ferns if you can get them.

71. Make a Tie/Dye Scarf or Handkerchief

Collect together:

A square of white sheeting or cotton about 14 ins. × 14 ins.
Dried peas
Strong thread
String
Packet of *cold* dye ⎫ Ask your mother to mix the dye ac-
Old bucket ⎬ cording to the instructions on the
Buttons ⎭ packet.
Needle and cotton
Scissors.

Now begin:

Place a button in the centre of the material then wrap the fabric over it, so that you can hold it tightly enclosed in the cloth (see diagram). Wind a piece of thread *very* tightly below the wrapped button; tie a knot so that it is firmly held in its new cloth cover. Tie peas firmly into the cloth knotting the thread afterwards so that it cannot possibly come undone. Tie buttons into the cloth in the same way at the four corners. Now drop the cloth into the bucket of cold dye and leave for 30 minutes. When you take it out, rinse it well under the cold tap, then unfasten all your wrappings. Hang the cloth out to dry, and ask your mother to iron it for you.

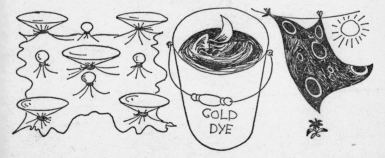

Where the string has been tied tightly the dye has been unable to soak through the cloth, so white circles should now decorate your fabric.

Turn the edges over twice and hem them very neatly as in the diagram. If you cannot hem, trim the edges with pinking shears so that they will not fray.

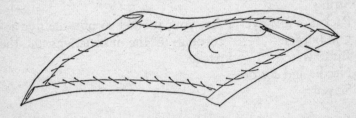

You could make a Tie/Dye bedspread for your doll's bed, or a traycloth for the kitchen tray. Make sure you measure the cloth to the right size before you start.

MAKING WITH MARZIPAN OR PASTRY

Packets of ready-made pastry and marzipan are available in all the shops, and ideal for all kinds of modelling ideas. Best point of all – you can eat your models afterwards!

72. Make a Marzi-man

Collect together:

½ lb. packet of ready-made marzipan
Rolling pin
Flour
2 currants
1 cherry
Cocktail stick or something pointed
Blunt knife.

Now begin:

Lightly sprinkle flour on your working surface. Roll and press the marzipan into a long oval shape – see Fig. 1. With the cocktail stick trace out your man, then carefully cut him out with the knife. Don't make his arms and legs too thin or they will drop off.

Press in two currants for his eyes. Use one half of the cherry for his nose, and cut the other half into quarters for his mouth (Fig. 2).

Make several Marzi-men when your friends are coming to tea.

Fig. 1   Fig. 2

73. Make Marzipan Fruit

Collect together:

A packet of marzipan – cut into 4 equal sections
Yellow and red colouring
A cheese grater
Knife
Cloves
Basin
Spoon
Greaseproof paper.

Now begin:

Make bananas

Take one section of marzipan and place it in the basin. Add three drops of yellow colouring. Mix well with spoon so that the marzipan is really yellow.

Roll out the marzipan on the greaseproof paper into a long sausage shape. Cut this into small pieces. Point the ends and twist into curved banana shapes.

Make oranges

Take another section of marzipan and colour it with 2 drops of red colouring and 2 drops of yellow. Mix well. Roll into

small balls on the greaseproof paper. Stick a clove, pointed end down, into the orange. Roll against a cheese grater very gently to make a rough skin surface.

Make lemons

Take another section of marzipan and colour it with 3 drops of yellow colouring. Mix well in the basin. Roll it into egg-shaped balls, and point the ends a little. Roll gently against the cheese grater to make a rough skin surface.

Make strawberries

Take the last section of marzipan. Colour it red. Roll into balls again but this time widen the top and point the bottom slightly. Flatten gently by pressing against the largest holed side of the cheese grater to get large circles in the strawberry skin.

Stick a clove into each strawberry for the stalk.

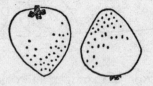

74. Make a Pastry Chain

Collect together:

  Packet of short pastry
  Baking tray.

Now begin:

Work on a lightly floured working top, and grease your baking tray before you begin.

Divide the pastry into eight pieces. Roll each section into a long firm strip. Roll the other pieces out to the same length. Join one strip into a ring and link the second strip through this ring. Repeat with all the lengths until you have a chain. Lift the chain carefully onto the baking tray, and ask your mother to cook it for you.

When crisp and golden brown eat with jam.

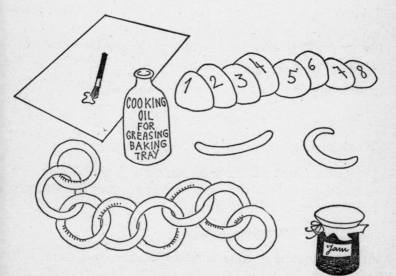

75. Make Pastry People

Collect together:

Packet of short pastry
Baking tray.

Now begin:

Work on a lightly floured working top.

Divide the pastry into sections, one for each member of your family. Flatten the pastry into different figures – for example, a father, mother and 2 children.

You can also make your pets.

Ask your mother to cook them for tea, and serve them with jam.

MAKE BELIEVE

Dressing up in a few old or interesting clothes can be great fun.

A dressing-up box filled with hats, clothes, beads, beards and suchlike can make you into a crowd of different characters. Here are a few ideas for 'pretending'.

76. Make Finger Puppets and a Theatre

Collect together:

Biro or felt pens
Matchbox.

Now begin:

Draw faces on the tips of your first and second fingers. Make them amusing, a happy face and a glum face.

Take the wrapper of a matchbox. Poke your fingers up inside the wrapper and act out your play, making your finger puppets move as they speak.

Stick hair on your puppets with glue if you want to add to their faces.

77. Make a Mask

Collect together:

Paper plate   Coloured pencils or paints
Scissors   Glue
String   Wool.
Pencil

Now begin:

Draw a face on the plate – eyes, mouth, nose and eyebrows.
Cut out the eyes and mouth. Make small holes at the edge of
the paper on a level with the eyes. Tie a length of string through
each hole.

Decorate the face with colours. Glue a fringe of wool lengths
on the forehead.

Tie the mask over your ears, so that it doesn't slip down.

78. Make a Play Sack

Collect together:

Crayons
Wool
A large paper bag
Scissors
Glue.

Now begin:

Place the paper bag over your head and decide where you will need the eye and mouth holes. Take it off and cut holes and a slit in the appropriate places. Decide what face you want for your play sack. Use wool for hair, beards, moustaches, manes, etc. Colour in cheeks, noses, ears and any other features you need.

Now pull the sack over your head, and act!

Remember! Always use a large PAPER bag. Polythene and plastic bags should never be used for a Play Sack.

PLEASE DO NOT USE PLASTIC BAGS

79. *Make a Secret Code*

Collect together:

Paper
Pencils
– and a friend or two.

Now begin:

Write the alphabet in a column. Now make up a sign for each letter and write it at the side. When you and your friends write letters to one another in the future, use the signs instead of ordinary words, and keep your messages a secret.

80. Make a Story Book

Collect together:

A zig-zag book – see 'Making with Paper' section
Label the front cover 'My Book of Stories'.

Now begin:

All sorts of events and ideas might prompt you to write a story. If you are a person who likes making things, keeping busy and thinking up ideas, you are sure to be a person with lots of stories in your head.

Try writing stories about events which have happened to you yourself. Put your ideas in your own way; most of all – use your imagination.

Write a holiday adventure about a holiday which goes absolutely wrong.

Write a frightening story based on something that has actually happened to you. Remember to say exactly how you felt at the time so that you make your reader just as frightened.

Write a story about a lucky escape. Get your hero into a really impossible and fantastic situation from which to free himself.

81. Make a Sock Puppet

Collect together:

An old white sock
Coloured felt pens.

Now begin:

Pull the sock over your left hand. Clench your fist, tucking any
spare sock under your fingers. With felt pen draw a face onto
the sock. Make this the face of any animal or insect you wish.
Make up an animal if the face turns out quite extraordinary.
The mouth will work best if drawn on a line with the top of
your thumb, and the eyes if on the knuckles of your first
finger. Practise making the face move into different expres-
sions. Invent a way of speaking for your puppet.

MAKING SOUNDS

Get together several of your friends and form a SCRATCH ORCHESTRA. You will need to make your own instruments so here are a few ideas.

A Bottle xylophone

You may already know how to obtain different notes from milk bottles filled with varying amounts of water. Try to make a scale, each note slightly higher than the last.

Which makes the lowest note?

Maraccas

Put a little rice or a few dried peas into a washing-up liquid bottle. Push the top tightly on again, or seal the opening with sticky tape.

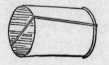

Shake fast and slow, soft and loud.

Tin drum

Stretch a rubber band round an empty cocoa tin. You don't need the tin lid on. Now 'plonk' on the rubber band where it is stretched over the open mouth of the tin.

Cymbals

Clash tin lids together.

Castanets

Knock wooden or metal spoons together.

Sound effects

Use your voice to make wheezing, gurgling and grinding sounds. If you are feeling particularly adventurous, join in with noises made with other parts of the body; rubbing palms together, clicking fingers, slapping thighs.

If you can record your orchestra on tape, add heavy breathing sounds into the microphone, or sprinkle grains of sand nearby for a pattering effect.

MAKING FOR CHRISTMAS

The best presents to give your family and friends at Christmas are those you have made yourself. Many of the ideas in this book would make small gifts, but here is an extra section, just for Christmas, with a few special ideas for mothers and fathers.

Always wrap your presents in bright paper and tie them with a pretty bow as this makes them look really special.

82. Make a Christmas Card

Collect together:

Stiff card
Scissors
Coloured tissues
Paste
Glitter.

Now begin:

Crease the card down the centre. Place it with the fold at the top – see diagram.

Cut sheets of different-coloured tissue into tree-shaped triangles of three sizes.

Spread a little paste on each triangle and glue to the card in your chosen design. Overlap some triangles for added effect, or crinkle some and add glitter, if you like, to make your trees sparkle.

83. Make a Cut-out Christmas Card

Collect together:

Stiff card   Sticky paper
Scissors   Glitter
Coloured crayons   Ribbons.
Pencil

Now begin:

Fold the card down the centre creasing it firmly, and place it with the fold at the top.

Draw on the card as in the diagrams above, according to the shape you want. Make sure your fold is part of the picture.

Cut out the shape, then decorate with crayons, glitter, sticky paper, etc., to make a really gay Christmas card.

84. Make a Gift-filled Balloon

Collect together:

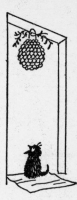

1 balloon
Small length of string or cord
Tissue paper
Newspaper ⎫
Paste ⎬ for papier mâché
Vaseline ⎭
Small wrapped gifts for the family.

Now begin:

Blow up the balloon. Knot the end when fairly large. Cover with papier mâché as for the Owl in the Papier Mâché section (No. 30).

Allow to dry for one to two days.

Burst the balloon and take it out. Cut the hole at the open end of the papier mâché, large enough to put your fist through.

Tie a knot in the cord and thread it through the papier mâché from one side of the opening to the other (see diagram).

Cut small circles of tissue and glue them to the balloon with a small dab of glue on the centre of the circle only. This will allow the circles to stick out away from the surface, and flutter when hung up.

Fill the balloon with gifts and hang in the room, or use it on its own as a Christmas decoration.

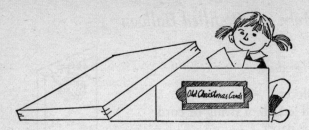

85. Make a Christmas Montage

Collect together:

Old Christmas cards
Scissors
Paste
Sheet of white card
Coloured Sellotape.

Now begin:

Cut out all the Santa Claus figures etc. you can find on the old cards. Arrange them on the card, so that they sometimes overlap. Paste them to the card, and frame your work neatly with coloured Sellotape.

86. Make a Pyramid Tree

This tree looks decorative and you can hide small presents inside it.

Collect together:

- 10 yoghourt pots
- Sticky paper
- Scissors

- Narrow coloured ribbon
- Strong glue
- Paste.

Now begin:

Cover the yoghourt pots with torn white paper pieces or simply wrap in glued or sticky white paper. Cut 10 Christmas trees the same size and colour in sticky-backed paper and stick on the front of the cups.

Decorate the wide rim of the cups with coloured ribbon. Glue it on or tie it round.

Pile the cups in a pyramid with the trees to the front.

Stick a cut-out star to a thin twig or stick and poke it through a small hole in the top cup.

Inside each cup put a surprise gift.

87. Make a Present for Your Mother

Collect together:

Empty, clean 1-pint cream carton.
Magazines
Scissors
Paste.

Gifts – tape measure, packet of pins, packet of needles, thimble, etc.

Now begin:

Cut out pictures of scissors, needles, materials, etc. from magazines. Paste them to the outside of the carton until the sides are completely covered.

Fill with gifts.

88. Make a Shell-box Present

Collect together:

A cardboard box, the size of a $\frac{1}{2}$ lb. box of chocolates
Shells
Strong glue
Length of braid or ribbon
Foil paper
Scissors
Varnish.

Now begin:

Cover the outside of the box with pieces of shiny foil paper glued into place.

Choose small, light-weight shells to glue onto the lid and arrange them in a decorative pattern.

Glue braid round the edge of the lid and the base of the box. When the glue is dry spray the box with clear varnish.

This makes a nice jewellery box for rings and bracelets.

89. Make a Shell Paperweight

Collect together:

    Polyfilla – mixed thickly in a basin
    Small shells and pebbles
    Large round, flat stone (clean)
    Varnish.

Now begin:

Cover the sides and top of the stone thickly with Polyfilla mix.
Arrange the shells and pebbles over it in a decorative pattern.
Leave to dry then spray with clear varnish.

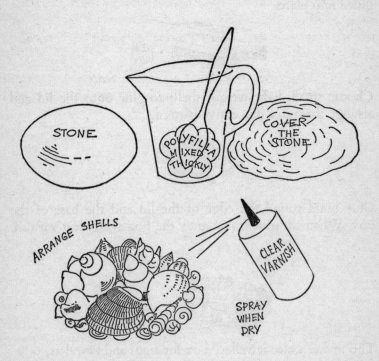

STONE

POLYFILLA MIXED THICKLY

COVER THE STONE

ARRANGE SHELLS

CLEAR VARNISH

SPRAY WHEN DRY

90. Make a Stable

Collect together:

> Corrugated paper 3 ins. wide by 16 ins. long
> Pine cones
> Strong glue
> Sellotape
> Sheet of strong card.

Now begin:

Bend the strip of corrugated paper 6 ins. from one end, to make an off-centre peak for the roof (Fig. 1).

Stand this bent section on the sheet of strong card and trace a triangle round it. Cut this out to make the back wall of the stable. Secure it to the corrugated roof with sellotape – inside, so that it does not show (Fig. 2).

Make roof tiles from pine-cone scales. Glue them on, starting at the bottom of the roof, and climbing to the peak row by row.

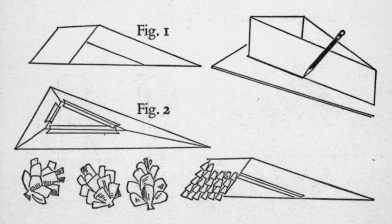

Fig. 1

Fig. 2

91. Make Figures for Your Stable

Collect together:

Sheets of newspaper
Cord
Wool
Sticky paper
Scraps of material
Strong glue.

Now begin:

Fold a sheet of newspaper 6 ins. by 12 ins. over and over into 2-inch wide folds. Double the folded length over and tie it at half height and three-quarter height. See diagram. Slip a narrower fold of paper between the ties for arms, and tie each of these at the wrist.

Open out the folds a little at the base of the figure so that it stands easily.

Decorate with wool hair, sticky-paper faces, and material robes and gowns.

Make the shepherds, Mary and Joseph.

92. Make a Toy-Box

Collect together:

A large cardboard box
About 6 egg cartons
Paint
Brushes
Crayon
Strong glue
Roll of old wallpaper
Wallpaper paste.

Now begin:

Inside the box

Tuck the box flaps firmly inside the box. Cut a strip of wallpaper that will completely cover the back, the base, and the front of the box and paste it on. Cut another strip which will cover the right side, the base, and the left side of the box and paste that on. The base will be doubly firm with these two paper layers covering it.

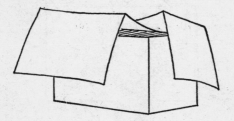

Outside the box

Mix a large quantity of a brightly coloured paint and brush it thickly over the four outside walls of the box. Turn the box so that the front is facing you.

Separate the individual egg cups from the cartons by tearing them gently apart. Draw in crayon a large monster which fills the front side of the box. Glue each cup and stick it firmly inside the outline of the monster. Make sure that each cup is as close as it will go to the others. Cover narrow parts of the monster's body with scales, small scraps torn from the lids of the egg cartons.

Choose a murky monster colour and paint the egg cups and scales very carefully. Paint round the sides of the egg cups as well as on top. Paint a bright eye or paste a shiny button on the monster's head.

93. Make a Knitting Bag

First make a fabric collage (No. 23). Use a piece of material at least 18 ins. × 14 ins.

If possible cut a second piece exactly the same size using the same fabric, but if not choose a backing fabric which matches a colour used in the collage.

Collect together:

> Fabric collage 18 ins. × 14 ins.
> Backing fabric 18 ins. × 14 ins.
> Cotton
> Needle
> Scissors
> Pins
> 2 handles (plastic or wooden).

Now begin:

Place the right sides of the collage and the backing fabric together, and pin them together as in Fig. 1. The pins should be about ½ in. from the edge of the fabric. Don't close the top of the bag and do remember to start pinning two ins. down from the top on each side.

Sew neatly round with a small running stitch. Start with a knot in the cotton and finish with a firm double stitch. Turn the bag to the right side.

Fig. 1

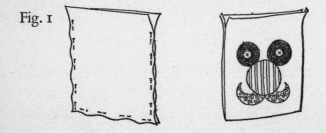

Slide the top edge of the collage through the handle and pin it down on the inside of the bag. Make a hem to hide any rough fraying edges and sew it neatly down. Do the same for the other handle (Fig. 2).

Fig. 2

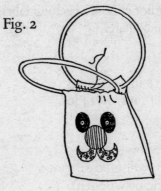

94. Make a Pressed-flower Calendar

You must prepare for this in the summer when the gardens are full of flowers and small, delicate wild flowers are growing along country roads. Choose neat, simple flowers whose petals will press out easily, interesting grasses and ferns. Lay them carefully between sheets of blotting paper or newspaper and press them under a pile of heavy books for about a week.

Collect together:

Pressed flowers
Glue
Coloured card
Small length of ribbon
Passe-partout or coloured sellotape
Calendar
Cellophane.

Now begin:

Select a few flowers, grasses and ferns which make a pleasing arrangement. Don't cram too much into the picture, a few simple flowers will make a better effect. Arrange them on the card as you plan to stick them. Leave a 1-inch margin round the edge. With small dabs of glue attach each flower to the card. Leave it to dry.

Cut a small piece of cellophane the size of the card and glue it round the edges. Stick it over the flowers. Cut 4 strips of passe-partout (2 as wide as the card and 2 as long as the card). Fold these strips in half, then glue them over the edges of the card to neaten and frame your picture.

Glue a loop of ribbon to the top centre of the card on the wrong side. Sellotape the calendar to the centre bottom, again on the wrong side.

We hope you have enjoyed this book. There are now more than 400 titles to choose from in the Puffin series, and some of them are described on the following pages.

SOMETHING TO DO

Septima

Here at last is a book to fill up all the wet days and dull days that produce the question 'What can I do?' in every family. *Something To Do* has more suggestions for things children can do at home, indoors and outside, without spending much money or being a terrible nuisance.

Each month has a separate chapter so that the games and ideas will fit in with the proper season. February, for instance, has a special section of Things To Do in Bed, and August, the holiday month, has a bunch of ideas to pass the time while travelling. Every month has its own special flower and bird to look for. There are tempting dishes to cook, things to make, games to play, and instructions for keeping pets. (*Original*)

THE PUFFIN SONG BOOK

Compiled and arranged by Leslie Woodgate

Whether you sing indoors or out, you will find something in this book for the mood and the moment.

There are some old favourites, and some songs you probably won't know at all, songs to sing alone and with other people. If you play the piano or the recorder or violin you will be able to try the accompaniments, and a few of the songs have percussion parts. (*Original*)

THE PUFFIN QUIZ BOOK (REVISED)

Norman and Margaret Dixon

What are the nine ways of getting out at cricket? What is meant by the classifications U, A and X for films? What do the Americans call petrol?

These are some of the four hundred questions and answers in the revised edition of *The Puffin Quiz Book*, which has been prepared from a selection of the most interesting questions in the two previous Puffin Quiz books. It is suitable for readers of ten to fifteen.

Also

THE JUNIOR PUFFIN QUIZ BOOK

Another collection by the same authors, Norman and Margaret Dixon, designed for younger readers. 1,000 questions on natural history, sport, geography and all kinds of general knowledge. (*Original*)

THE PUFFIN CROSSWORD PUZZLE BOOK

Alan Cash

A hundred crossword puzzles for children aged 9 to 13, some general and some on animals, famous people, history, books – even a section on other Puffins. (*Original*)

THE PUFFIN BOOK OF MAGIC

Norman Hunter

The magic in this book will not enable you to turn your schoolteacher into a chocolate-cream frog, or cause a mighty palace to arise in the back garden. But it does show you how to perform exciting, amusing, mysterious and somewhat joyous conjuring tricks, to entertain your friends and cause them to think you no end of a clever chap (or girl, of course). It also shows you how to have a bit of fun making some of the things used in the tricks, without also making too much mess.

Norman Hunter, who conjured up the Professor Branestawm stories, has included several tricks that he performs in his own Chinese magic act, which he lets off under the name of Ho Wat Fun. (*Original*)

THE YOUNG PUFFIN BOOK OF VERSE

compiled by Barbara Ireson

This is a collection of poems, verses, nursery rhymes and
jingles for children up to the age of eight. It is an introduction
to a vast heritage of poetry. Though diverse in form, language,
mood and subject, each poem has been chosen with care as
being within the grasp of young readers and listeners.

There are poems included by writers whose names are
bywords in the world of children's literature: Edward Lear,
Kate Greenaway and Walter de la Mare, as well as many
poems by writers whose names are normally found only in
collections for adults: Robert Frost, W. B. Yeats, and James
Kirkup. All the poets with whom modern children are
familiar are here too, including James Reeves, Rachel Field,
Eleanor Farjeon and Leonard Clark. Finally, there are also
many anonymous poems. (*Original*)

and for younger brothers and sisters ...

THIS LITTLE PUFFIN...

compiled by Elizabeth Matterson

A treasury of finger plays and singing and action games, which
will be a delight for anyone who wishes to persuade young
children to join in musical activities, either in groups or
individually. Each of the items has been well tried and
proved popular since this collection was compiled with the
help of nursery schools all over the country. (*Original*)

If you have enjoyed this book and would like to know about others which we publish, why not join the Puffin Club? You will receive the club magazine, *Puffin Post*, four times a year and a smart badge and membership book. You will also be able to enter all the competitions. For details, send a stamped addressed envelope to:

The Puffin Club Dept. A
Penguin Books Limited
Bath Road
Harmondsworth
Middlesex